T0222012

尾 田 栄 一 郎

Here's volume 10. It's been two years since I started this series. Two years...two years... Back then Sazae-san, who's 24, was only 24... Oh, now that I think about it, I'm now the same age as Sazae-san. But it seems like I used to be the same age as Katsuo-kun. Who will it be next? Norisuke-kun? Taiko-san? Tara-san? It makes me laugh to say "Tara-san." Or "Ikura-san." What am I going on about? Anyway, I'm the same as ever—not working, just drawing manga.

-Eiichiro Oda, 1999

Editor's note: The aforementioned names belong to ageless characters from the beloved cartoon series, *Sazae-san.*

Eiichiro Oda began his manga career at the age of 17, when his one-shot cowboy manga **Wanted!** won second place in the coveted Tezuka manga awards. Oda went on to work as an assistant to some of the biggest manga artists in the industry, including Nobuhiro Watsuki, before winning the Hop Step Award for new artists. His pirate adventure **One Piece**, which debuted in **Weekly Shonen Jump** in 1997, quickly became one of the most popular manga in Japan.

ONE PIECE VOL. 10
EAST BLUE PART 10

SHONEN JUMP Manga Edition

This volume contains material that was originally
published in English in **SHONEN JUMP** #36–38.

STORY AND ART BY EIICHIRO ODA

English Adaptation/Lance Caselman
Translation/Naoko Amemiya
Touch-up Art & Lettering/Mark McMurray
Additional Touch-up/Josh Simpson
Design/Sean Lee
Editor/Yuki Takagaki

Printed in Italy

Published by VIZ Media, LLC
P.O. Box 77010
San Francisco, CA 94107

25
First printing, April 2006
Twenty-fifth printing, July 2024

viz.com

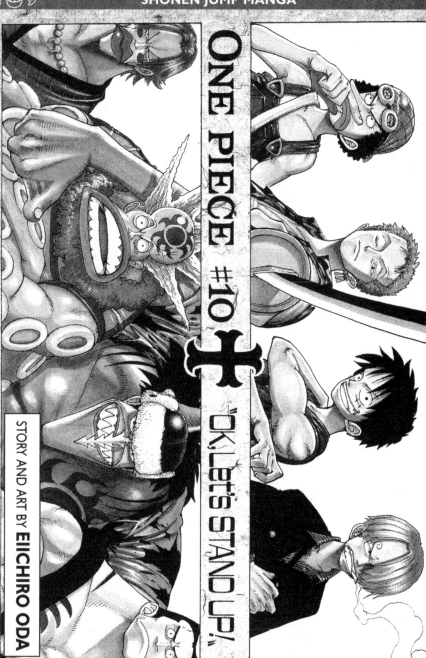

ONE PIECE #10

"OK, Let's Stand Up!"

STORY AND ART BY EIICHIRO ODA

Genzo

Nojiko

"Red-Haired" Shanks

THE STORY OF ONE PIECE
Volume 10

Monkey D. Luffy started out as just a kid with a dream — and that dream was to become the greatest pirate in history! Stirred by the tales of pirate "Red-Haired" Shanks, Luffy vowed to become a pirate himself. That was before the enchanted Devil Fruit gave Luffy the power to stretch like rubber, at the cost of being unable to swim — a serious handicap for an aspiring sea dog. Undeterred, Luffy set out to sea and recruited some crewmates: lying sharpshooter Usopp, master swordsman Zolo, and treasure-hunting thief Nami.

Luffy and his shipmates have finally defeated Don Krieg and his pirates and added the high-kicking cook Sanji to their crew. At last it seems they can finally set sail for the Grand Line—until they discover that their navigator, Nami, has deserted! Zolo and Usopp sail after her and come upon an island under the tyrannical rule of the fiendish Fish-Man Pirates and their leader, Captain "Saw-Tooth" Arlong. Worse still, Nami is in cahoots with them.

Luffy and the others reach the island, but despite what they hear about Nami they refuse to believe it. They come to understand Nami's hatred of pirates when they learn from her foster sister, Nojiko, that their adoptive mother, Belle-Mère, was killed by Arlong. They discover, too, that Nami has been hoarding her loot to buy Coco Village back from Arlong. Nami, who has been fighting a solitary battle for so long, finally asks Luffy for help.

Kuroobi

Sanji
The kind-hearted cook (and ladies' man) whose dream is to find the legendary sea, the "All Blue."

Hatchan (Hachi)

Nami
A thief who specializes in robbing pirates. Nami hates pirates, but Luffy convinced her to join his crew as navigator.

Monkey D. Luffy
Boundlessly optimistic and able to stretch like rubber, he is determined to become the King of the Pirates.

Roronoa Zolo
A former bounty hunter and master of the "three-sword" fighting style. He plans to become the world's greatest swordsman!

Usopp
A village boy with a talent for telling tall tales. His father, Yasopp, is a member of Shanks's crew.

Arlong

Choo

Vol. 10
OK, Let's STAND UP!

CONTENTS

8

YOU'D BETTER STOP...

SWUP

FIRST YOU GOTTA TELL US YOUR STORY.

HEH HEH HEH. STOP RIGHT THERE.

WHERE DO YOU THINK YOU'RE GOING?

AYE...

SHFF

SHFF SHFF

KR

OUTTA MY WAY.

!!?

WHAT BUSINESS DO YOU HAVE WITH ME, PIRATE?

SHFF SHFF SHFF...

KERPLONK!

HEY !!

!

12

WHAT'S THIS!?

YOU SEE HIM SEND THAT MONSTER ARLONG FLYING!?

HE CAN'T BE A NORMAL HUMAN!!

YACK YACK

HEY!! JUST WHO ARE THOSE GUYS!?

IF YOU INSIST ON BUTTING INTO THIS FIGHT, YOU'LL HAVE TO GO THROUGH US!!

YOU'LL ONLY BE GETTING IN OUR COMRADES' WAY HERE.

YOU CAN'T DEFEAT THE FISH-MEN YOUR-SELVES.

THAT'S A GOOD ENOUGH REASON FOR US TO RISK OUR LIVES.

DO-OM!!

THEY MADE SISTER NAMI CRY.

DOOM!!

YOU HAVE NO REASON TO FIGHT!

WHY ARE YOU DOING THIS?

HA HA HA HA!! YOU'RE JUST FOUR PEOPLE FROM AN INFERIOR SPECIES.

WHAT CAN YOU DO!!?

YOU MEAN TO TELL ME...

...YOU CAME HERE FOR NAMI?

NO!!!

WHAT?

ARISE, GIANT WARRIOR !!!

TOOT-TOOT-TOOOT! TOOT-TOOOT!

DO YOU BONEHEADS THINK...

...YOU CAN PUSH LORD ARLONG AROUND? I'LL TURN YOU INTO CHUM!!!

THE ONE THAT DECIMATED GOSA!!

OOOOO

THE MONSTER FROM THE GRAND LINE!!

AGH! WHAT IS IT!!?

AAAAAAH

OH, IT'S JUST HIM.

SO HE WORKS FOR THESE GUYS.

WHERE ARE YOU GOING !!?

WAIT, MOMOO !!

SWOOO ~~~......SH

MOO...

MOO-HOO !!!

WHAT DO YOU THINK YOU'RE DOING?

MOMOO ?

...I WON'T STOP YOU.

WELL, IF YOU WANT TO RUN AWAY...

shake shake shake shake

GO AHEAD, MOMOO.

HERE HE COMES!!!!

19

GRAAAH!!!

TOMP!!!

MOOOO!!!

KRAKK...!!

SHFF

TOMP!!!

WHUPWHUPWHUP

NUMPH!!

WAH!!

WHUPWHUP

I HAVE A BAD FEELING ABOUT THIS.

WHAT'S HE DOING?

I CAME HERE TO CLOBBER ...

I DIDN'T COME HERE TO WASTE TIME ON SMALL FRY!!

... YOU !!!!

I WAS JUST THINKING ABOUT CLOBBERING YOU, TOO.

WELL THAT WORKS OUT PERFECTLY.

SMEK. ♡

I'LL SHOW YOU THAT HUMANS ARE NO MATCH FOR FISH-MEN!

WHAT HE DID TO OUR COMRADES WASN'T NICE!!!

LOOKS LIKE WE'LL HAVE TO GET INVOLVED.

DO-DOOM!!

YOU'LL GET US ALL IN TROUBLE!!

THWAK THWAK!

HUH!?

HUH!?

CONSIDER THE DANGER, YOU FOOL!!

NOW THE REAL PLAYERS APPEAR.

GRRR...

Q: This is Timmy Ueda of the SBS Takeover Gang!
I'm going to begin the SBS Question Corner before you do,
Oda Sensei!!
SBS will now begin!!

A: AGh! Oh no, you did it!
Darn you, Timmy.
Now I can't do it! Well, I guess it's already begun.

Q: Hello, Oda Sensei. On page 92 of volume 8, in panel
6, it says "Find Panda Man," but I can't find him.
Where is he?

A: Oh, that. I got a lot of postcards
about that. Some people found
him and some didn't. First of all,
I didn't even expect people to
notice those tiny words.
Nevertheless, I'll give the answer.
Inside the lower circle, it does
indeed say, "Find Panda Man!!!" And
Panda Man can be seen in the
circle at the upper right.

THANKS FOR THE BOAT. CAN WE KEEP IT?

KREEK...⋯!!

SEE YOU AROUND.

WE'LL SINK !!

WE'LL SINK !!

(THE SCENE IN QUESTION)

Find Panda Man!!!

← Close-up, lower left

Close-up, upper right →

◄ He's making a peace sign.

Chapter 83:
LUFFY IN BLACK

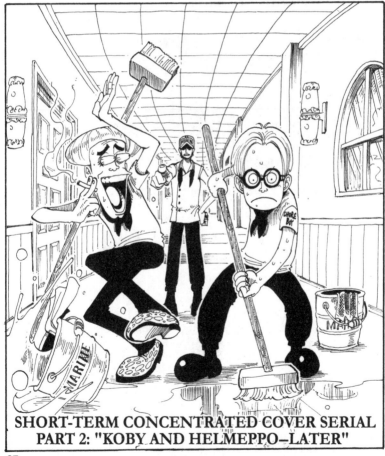

**SHORT-TERM CONCENTRATED COVER SERIAL
PART 2: "KOBY AND HELMEPPO—LATER"**

OOOOOO...

LET'S SEE WHAT THESE GUYS CAN DO.

VEEN

klik klikklik...

A HUMAN WHO'S A MATCH FOR THE FISH-MEN.

DA-DOOM!!

WE SHOULD'VE CRUSHED THESE HUMANS AS SOON AS THEY SHOWED UP!

...YOU'LL DESTROY ARLONG PARK!!

SMEK. ♥

IF YOU LOSE YOUR TEMPER...

.....

LORD ARLONG, PLEASE DON'T GET WORKED UP.

YEAH!!

THERE'S A LITTLE PROBLEM, GUYS...

OCTOPUS SHOULD BE BOILED IN SALT WATER, SLICED, AND SEASONED WITH OLIVE OIL AND PAPRIKA. IT'S GREAT WITH BOOZE.

THAT OCTOPUS IS UP TO SOMETHING.

TIME FOR...

ZERO VISIBILITY.

DOOM

FLOOSH

HACHI INK JET!!!

BLINK

HUH?

INK JET...

HACHI...

...ON THE ROCKS!!!!

KR AK!

I'VE ENTERED THE FRAY ON BEHALF OF THAT FOOL OF A CAPTAIN.

HOORAY, SANJI!

WHAT HAVE I DONE?

KA-BOOS!!!

KLAK.

KLAK. KLAK..

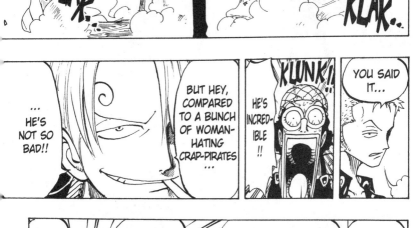

...HE'S NOT SO BAD!!

BUT HEY, COMPARED TO A BUNCH OF WOMAN-HATING CRAP-PIRATES...

HE'S INCRED-IBLE!!

KLUNK!!

YOU SAID IT...

STILL?

MY FEET STILL WON'T COME OUT!

HUH?

...BUT THAT WAS A RATHER GALLANT ACT FOR A PIRATE.

YOU'RE PRETTY STRONG, FOR A HUMAN...

WAAAAH!!!

WHOOM

I'LL SMASH YOU!!!

C'MON, LUFFY! TRY POINTING YOUR TOES!!

TMP TMP TMP TMP TMP

!?

HEY, OCTO-PUS.

THEY'RE BUSY RIGHT NOW.

KREK

KREK...!!

I ALMOST FORGOT ABOUT YOU!!

GRRR!!

RORONOA ZOLO!!

WHY DON'T YOU SMASH ME?

YOU MUST REALLY WANT ME TO HURT YOU!!

AAAAAAAAH!!!

WAAAAAAAAH!!!

TMP TMP TMP TMP

SHOOM!!!

BROTHER USOPP!!

....!!

JUDGING FROM THE WEAPONS YOU'RE HOLDING...

AND THAT MEANS THAT EVERY ONE OF YOU HAS TO...

...I'D SAY THIS IS A REBELLION.

YOU'RE FROM COCO VILLAGE, AREN'T YOU?

SMEK. ♡

HEY, DIDN'T YOU GUYS COME HERE TO CHALLENGE US?

YOU'RE STILL HERE?

HE'S ONE OF THE PIRATES TOO?

ISN'T HE THE GUY THAT SAVED GENZO AT THE VILLAGE?

41

WAP!!

DO YOU FOOLS ACTUALLY THINK YOU CAN BEAT US?

...SOMETHING YOU WANT TO SAY? IS THERE...

NOW LET GO OF MY HAND!!

DARN RIGHT WE DO!!

YEAH, WE ACTUALLY DO.

KRAK KRAK

KRAK

!? WHAM!!

NO...NO THANKS!!

42

EXCELLENT PLAN.

FINISH THESE CUSTOMERS OFF, THEN DRAG HIM OUT?

THERE'S ONLY ONE WAY TO RESCUE LUFFY!!

JUMPING INTO THE OCEAN IS JUST WHAT THEY WANT US TO DO!!!

HA HA HA HA HA!!

TIME TO PLAY, EH?

YEAH!!!

LET'S DO IT!!!

KLANK!!

WOOOOO

AAAAAH!!

GLUB GLUB

THIS IS BAD. I HAVE NO STRENGTH...

Q: When Arlong and the other Fish-Men have children, do they lay eggs like fish do?

A: (Buzz) The Fish-Men are actually mammals, so they have kids the same way humans do. Of course, that's the job of the Fish-Women.

Q: I, like, totally wanna know the heights of the crew. That Nami is, like, soooo cute!

A: The main five, eh? All right. Um, first of all, Gaimon's height is... Just kidding. Okay, I'll start with the shortest. Nami's 5' 6 ½", Luffy is 5' 8," Usopp is 5' 8½", Sanji is a little under 5' 10," and Zolo is 5' 10." So basically, they're all like about the same height.

Q: Of the Fish-Men, Hatchan is the cutest and funniest. So what I wonder is, how come his full name is Hatchan and his nickname is Hachi? (In Japanese, "-chan" is usually part of a nickname.)

A: You know how Chinese people sometimes have Chan as a last name? It's kind of the same thing.

Q: What is that thing wrapped around the waists of Usopp and most of the pirates that appear in *One Piece*? A towel? Or are they trying to copy Zolo's haramaki?

A: ← You mean this? Yeah, they're all wearing it, huh. But there's no deep significance to it. It's just a sash. It seems that pirates liked to wear them. But they used to stick pistols and knives in them, so they aren't just for show.

Chapter 84:
ZOMBIE

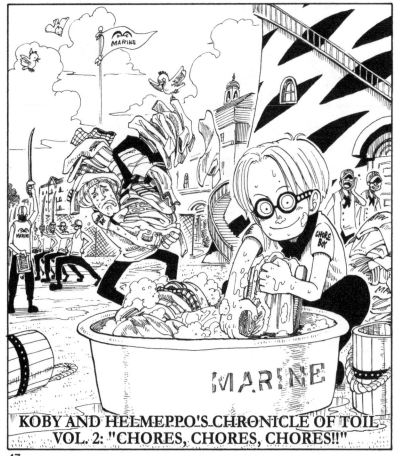

KOBY AND HELMEPPO'S CHRONICLE OF TOIL
VOL. 2: "CHORES, CHORES, CHORES!!"

EEK!!! MY HAIR!!!

HMPH.

UM... THANKS?

...YOU'RE ABSOLUTELY RIGHT!!! HEY, IT'S ONLY HAIR! IT'LL GROW BACK!!

IF YOU THINK I'LL LET YOU GET AWAY WITH THAT...

HUMAN SCUM!!!

52

THE PAIN!! MY LUNGS ARE BURSTING!!

TUM—...P!!

SEE, RORONOA ZOLO!? I'M MORE THAN A MATCH FOR ANY SWORDSMAN.

NOW DO YOU GET IT!?

...SWORD CATCH!!!

FWASH!!

HACHI'S TRIPLE...

YEAH, YOU TALK A LOT!!!

I HEARD YOU USE A THREE-SWORD STYLE.

SO WHY ONLY ONE SWORD!?

STOP STALLING !!!

WHAT THE HECK!? GET DOWN HERE!!!

DA——DOOM

• • •

SHUT UP!! I'M NOT EVEN TRYING!!!

YOU'RE LOSING PLENTY AGAINST JUST ONE SWORD, FISH!!

GLUB

GLUB

... A HUMAN SWORDSMAN CAN NEVER BEAT ME!!!

THERE'S A REASON WHY...

WE'VE GOT TO DO SOMETHING TO SAVE HIM!!

BUT AT THIS RATE, BROTHER LUFFY'S DOOMED!!

BUT IF WE DIVE INTO THE OCEAN NOW, THEY'LL JUST DRAG US TO THE BOTTOM!!

DARN!! THAT SLIPPERY OCTOPUS CLOWN IS WASTING OUR PRECIOUS TIME!!

MR. GENZO...

I'LL GO HELP THAT YOUNG RUBBER BOY.

YOU THINK YOU CAN ACCOMPLISH ANYTHING IN THE OCEAN, INJURED LIKE YOU ARE!?

BUT...

KLIK

KLIK

THROB

THROB

OUCH!!!

WAIT FOR US!!

TUP

ZING!!

AND ME!!

COUNT ME IN!

ME TOO, MR. GENZO.

I'LL GO, TOO!!

BUT, MR. GENZO!

I'LL GO ALONE!!

...AND THE RUBBER BOY AND HIS FRIENDS WILL HAVE FOUGHT FOR NOTHING.

THAT'S AN ORDER.

IF THE FISH-MEN SPOT A CROWD OF US IN THE WATER, THEY'LL ATTACK...

NO!!

IT'S MY LITTLE SISTER THOSE GUYS ARE FIGHTING FOR!

NOJIKO!! BUT YOUR STOMACH...

MR. GENZO, I'M GOING TOO!!

WE'LL LEAVE YOU TO IT! BUT HURRY!

GOOD LUCK!!

RIGHT!!

COME ON!! WE HAVE TO HURRY!!

TMP TMP!!

WHOOM

...!!

...!!

DO YOU KNOW WHY NO HUMAN COULD EVER BEAT ME?

FWUMP...

WHAT !?

HUH !?

KLAK KLANK

FWO ON...!!

HUH!?

WH

AH HA HA HA!

AP!!

?

KA-B L O SH

HUFF...

HUFF...

HUFF...

AAAAAGH!!!

I'LL CRUSH YOU.

I THOUGHT IT WAS STRANGE THAT HE COULD GET CUT UP LIKE THAT AND RECOVER SO FAST!!

THAT STUPID IDIOT.

OF COURSE! THEY WOULD'VE KILLED ANY NORMAL MAN-- OR AT LEAST CRIPPLED HIM FOR HALF A YEAR!!

SO THOSE WOUNDS WERE TOO DEEP, AFTER ALL...

OUR BROTHER'S BEEN SUFFERING IN SILENCE ALL THIS TIME!!

FWUMP!!

twitch

CRAP...

WHY NOW OF ALL TIMES!?

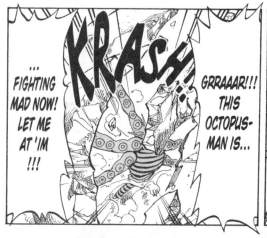

...FIGHTING MAD NOW! LET ME AT 'IM!!!

KRASH!!

GRRAAAR!!! THIS OCTOPUS-MAN IS...

HOW LONG ARE YOU GONNA SLEEP!?

HACHI!! WAKE UP!!

NO MERE HUMAN COULD EVER BEAT ME, EVEN IF HEAVEN AND EARTH TURNED UPSIDE DOWN!!!

I'M THE SECOND BEST SWORDS-MAN ON FISH-MAN ISLAND!! THEY CALL ME HACHI OF THE SIX-SWORD STYLE!!! DID YOU KNOW THAT!!?

SIX-SWORD STYLE? SOUNDS SILLY.

IS THAT FOR CHOPPING VEGETABLES!?

WHO ARE YOU GOING TO FIGHT, HACHI?

HUH?

HUH!!?

...NO ONE CAN TAKE MY LIFE!!!

LISTEN UP, OCTOPUS!!

THERE'S A MAN I HAVE TO MEET, AND UNTIL I SEE HIM AGAIN...

I'LL KILL YOU, RORONOA ZOLO!!!

HE'S ALIVE, EH?

YEAH, ZOLO!!!

YOSAKU, JOHNNY...YOUR SWORDS!

NOW I'LL SHOW YOU THE THREE-SWORD STYLE.

HMPH. THAT'S IT?

WHP WHP

TUMP!!

GULP..!!

...!!

EWIK

...THEN THOSE KICKS THE CRAP-GEEZER USED TO LAY ON ME MUST'VE BEEN 400TH DEGREE.

PLIP...

IF THAT WAS A 40TH-DEGREE PUNCH...

TMP TMP!

AAAAAAAAAH!!!

GLUB

GLUB

Q: Here goes! Oooone! Twoooo!! Threeeee!!!

A: **Thump!!!!**

Q: One more time! ♡ Oooone.♡ Twoooo.♡ Threeeee.♡

A: **Thump!!!** Oh... I'm being played.

Q: Yo! Wassup? ONE PIECE is A-OK! It's always lots of fun and a regular storm of emotions. This is my first time writing to a manga artist. ♡ Oda Sensei, you're a character I like.

A: I'm not a character.

Q: The other day a friend asked me to draw Shanks, so I did. Then suddenly my friend hit me on the head and said, "How come you drew Django!?" Am I sick?

A: Yes. It's an illness. It's "Django Drawer's Disease." You just keep drawing Django. Late-stage symptoms include drawing Django even when you're signing for deliveries, so please be careful.

Q: That thing that's perched on Zeff's head on page 121 of volume 8 is a hat, right? My mom won't believe me. She says, "It's too tall to be a hat. There must be a pole behind him." Sensei, please tell her yourself so the blockhead (age 44) will believe it.

A: Er, Mom, please listen carefully. In this world, there are facts that cannot be bent and realities from which we cannot avert our eyes. The thing that looms above Zeff's head is a "Tower of Faith" that rises up because of his spirit. It is called the "Blue Heavens-Dividing Chef's Hat!" It's true!!!!

Chapter 85:
THREE SWORDS VS. SIX

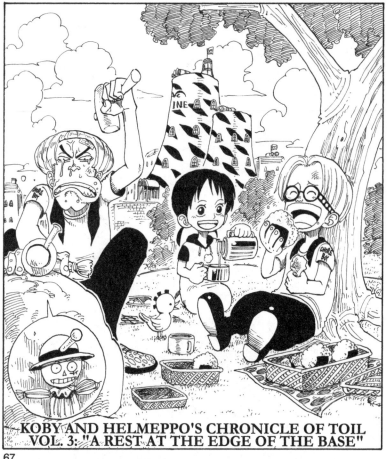

KOBY AND HELMEPPO'S CHRONICLE OF TOIL
VOL. 3: "A REST AT THE EDGE OF THE BASE"

FWIP
FWIP

FWIP
FWIP

WHOOSH!!

CATCH, BROTHER !!!

WE THREW THEM TO YOU!! CATCH THEM!!!

FWIP FWIP
FWIP
FWIP

BROTHER!! OUR SWORDS!!

THIS IS BAD... I'M ABOUT TO PASS OUT. AND MY FEVER, INSTEAD OF GOING DOWN, IS RISING!!

HUFF... HUFF...

BROTHER ZOLO, LOOK OUT!!!

FWIP FWIP

FWIP WIP

Wobble   Wobble

THIS IS THE *SIX-SWORD* STYLE, WHICH CAN ONLY BE PERFORMED BY SOMEONE WITH SIX ARMS AND A CHARMINGLY FLEXIBLE BODY.

CHO   OM!!

I'LL SHOW YOU A WORLD THAT NO TWO-ARMED HUMAN CAN ENTER !!!

JUST THINK ABOUT IT MATHEMATICALLY. THREE BLADES...

...IS THE MAXIMUM YOU CAN HOLD. YOU HAVE NO CHANCE AGAINST MY SIX BLADES.

I'M GOING TO CHOP YOU UP!!!

WHY DO YOU FIGHT SO HARD WHEN YOU CANNOT WIN?

WHAT DRIVES YOU?

THAT WOULD BE A GRAVE MISCALCULATION.

MATHEMATICALLY!?

THEY'RE MUCH WEIGHTIER THAN YOURS ARE!!!

I MAY ONLY HAVE THREE BLADES, BUT LOOK AT THEM!

WO oo oo o ooOO

DARN IT! I DON'T KNOW IF THIS WILL WORK ON THE OCEAN FLOOR!!!

KLANG

GLUG

HE'S SWALLOWED AN AWFUL LOT OF WATER!! IF WE CAN'T FREE HIM SOON, IT'LL BE TOO LATE!!

GLUG

KLANG

GLUG

THE WATER'S BUOYANCY IS TOO STRONG!!

GLUG

KLANG!!

GLUG

I NEED AN OXYGEN TANK, BUT THERE'S NO TIME TO GET ONE!!

AND I CAN'T CARRY HIM TO THE SURFACE WITH THE THING ATTACHED!!

IT'S NO USE! I CAN'T BREAK THE ROCK!!!

HURRY!

MR. GENZO...

THAT'S IT!!

GLUG

74

AND HE EVEN MANAGED TO CUT UP MY HANDS!

THAT HUMAN MATCHED THE ROTATION OF MY BLADES AND PASSED RIGHT BETWEEN THEM!

WELL I'M A SWORDSMAN, NOT AN ACROBAT !!!

YOSAKU, ALL THIS FIGHTING'S SURE TO OPEN UP BROTHER ZOLO'S WOUNDS!!

WHAT COULDA HAPPENED!!?

HOW !?

HUH !!?

THWUMP.

BROTHER ZOLO LOOKS LIKE HE'S IN PAIN!!

I'D TRADE PLACES WITH HIM IF I COULD.

HUFF

HUFF

Plup plup...

KLAN---G

OH, NOW I'VE REALLY HAD IT WITH YOU! I'M REALLY GONNA KILL YOU!!!

KLAN---G!!

...OCTOPUS POT STANCE !!! YOU'RE AS GOOD AS DEAD !!!

SIX-SWORD STYLE...

...I CANNOT FALL.

EVEN IF MOST PEOPLE WOULD PASS OUT FROM WOUNDS LIKE THESE...

Plup plup

FWOOSH!!!

THIS TECHNIQUE IS 100% UNSTOPPABLE!!!

IT ALREADY WORKED ON YOU ONCE!!!

...I CANNOT DIE.

EVEN IF THESE WOUNDS WOULD KILL MOST PEOPLE...

WHEEZE

KLA-KU

NEW YEAR'S...

--GIRI!!!

ANG!!!

I CANNOT FALL.

I HAVE TO LIVE TO DEFEAT "HAWK-EYE" MIHAWK.

SW UP...

ONI--

SRIK SRIK...

HUH...?

EH, OCTOPUS BOY!? ARE YOU SATISFIED!?

NOW DO YOU SEE WHOSE SWORDS ARE WEIGHTIER?

DRAGON...

HE COULDN'T HAVE...

HACHI! ...

HOW... COULD I LOSE TO ONLY THREE SWORDS?

WHA-KRASH!!

THE REST OF YOU ARE BENEATH MY NOTICE.

I HAVE TO SAVE LUFFY!!

KRAK

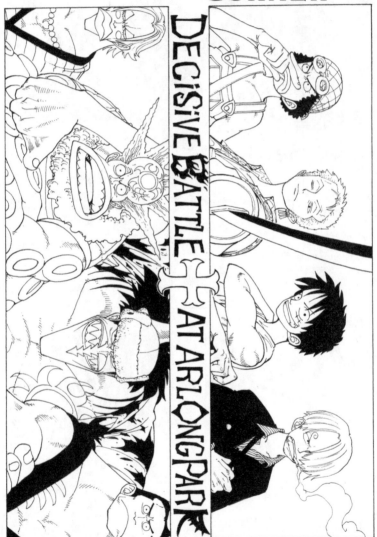

DECISIVE BATTLE AT ARLONG PARK

Chapter 86:
HEROISM VS.
FISH-MAN CRUELTY

STOP, ZOLO!!

IF YOU GO INTO THE OCEAN LIKE THAT YOU'LL DIE!!

WHUP···!!!

HAVE TO HURRY... LUFFY...

I CAN'T WAIT AROUND FOR YOU TO FIGHT!!

I KNOW!!

SHUT UP!! LUFFY'S GOT TO BE AT HIS LIMIT BY NOW!!

I'M STOPPING YOU BECAUSE I KNOW THAT ALL TOO WELL, CRAP-SWORDSMAN!!

I KNOW THERE'S NO TIME.

WHAT!? ISN'T THAT...

...THE VILLAGE HEADMAN !!?

!?

DO

OM!!

GLUB

GLUB

IS THAT LUFFY'S STRETCHED NECK!?

HURRY, BEFORE MY BREATH RUNS OUT...

WUMP

WUMP

PLEASE LET US BE IN TIME!!!

C'MON, BREATHE!!

WHUMP

WHUMP

...WITH THIS STRETCHY NECK OF YOURS, YOU COULD AT LEAST COUGH UP WATER AND BREATHE!!

I'M SORRY!! I DON'T HAVE THE STRENGTH TO BRING UP YOUR WHOLE BODY, BUT...

THAT'S IT, MR. GENZO!!

YES !!

PLOOSH

WHUMP

WHUMP

...AND LEAVE THE REST TO THE OLD MAN!!

GLUB GLUB

THEN I JUST HAVE TO SHATTER THE ROCK WITH A KICK...

GLUB

GLUB

GOOD. NOW EVEN WITH HIS FEET IN THE ROCK, HE CAN AT LEAST BREATHE !!

FISH-MAN KARATE ...

FOREARM SLEDGE !!!

!!?

HMPH, IT'S THOSE WORMS FROM COCO VILLAGE! BUT THEY'RE WASTING THEIR TIME !!

....!!!

BLOOP!!

!?

I'LL DROWN YOU RIGHT NOW !!!

GLUB GLUB GLUB

DO YOU REALLY THINK YOUR EFFORTS...

...WILL BUY YOU ANY MORE TIME IN THIS WORLD !?

I'VE BEEN SPOTTED BY A FISH-MAN!!

GLUB

OH NO !!

GLUB

NOT IF I CAN HELP IT!!

IT'LL BE ALL YOU CAN DO JUST TO HOLD YOUR BREATH, HUMAN!!

YOU WANT TO FIGHT *ME* UNDERWATER!?

...!!

THE DUELLING HAIR TETHER!!!

ALL RIGHT, THEN. I'LL TAKE YOU ON!!

FLAMING AXE KICK !!!

GLUB ...!!

KRAK!!

BACK FOOT JAW-BREAKER !!!

....!!

UNGH!! I LET OUT TOO MUCH AIR!! I NEED AIR! AIR!!

FWUP
FWUP
FWUP
FWUP
FWUP
FWUP
FWUP
FWUP
FW

BOOM!

!

SW

OPS

PLOOF!!!

H!!

WHERE ARE YOU GOING?

YOUR ABILITY TO TAKE PUNISHMENT IS ANNOYING. IT'S NOT NORMAL FOR A HUMAN.

GLUB

CRAP!!! LET ME PASS!!! AIR!!! I GOTTA BREATHE!!!

YOU WANT TO ESCAPE FROM ME, BUT YOU CAN'T.

GLUB

GLUB

BUT LET ME EXPLAIN TO YOU THE CONSEQUENCES OF YOUR FOOLHARDY HEROISM!!!

THIS GAME ENDS IN ONLY ONE WAY... DEATH.

!!

THEN I'LL FINISH OFF THAT LONG-NOSED FOOL AND ZOLO, AND I'LL KILL ALL THE VILLAGERS FOR THEIR REBELLION!!

THE RUBBER MAN WILL DIE AT THE SAME TIME.

....!!

AND WHEN YOU'RE FINISHED, I'LL KILL THE VILLAGE HEADMAN.

IN THE END, YOUR HEROISM IS JUST SO MUCH HOT AIR.

TREMBLE...

AND AFTER ALL THIS, I CAN'T VERY WELL LET THAT TRAITOR NAMI GET AWAY, CAN I !!?

IT CAN'T SAVE A SINGLE SOUL!!!

!!!!

DO YOU UNDER-STAND?

...YOUR GUTS WOULD BE SQUEEZED OUT OF YOUR BODY!!!

IF YOU WERE TO DESCEND RAPIDLY TO THE BOTTOM OF THE OCEAN...

SHWAP...!!

YOU HUMANS TRULY ARE POWERLESS CREATURES.

YOU CAN'T EVEN ENDURE EXTREME CHANGES IN WATER PRESSURE!!

!

THE OLD MAN WILL HAVE TO TAKE CARE OF LUFFY FOR NOW.

GOTTA CHANGE THE PLAN!!

SWOOSH

PULVERIZING PRESSURE PLUNGE!!!

CRUNK

!!!

AH HA HA HA HA!!!

HE THINKS I CAN'T SAVE ANYONE!?

I WON'T LET HIM GET AWAY WITH THIS!!!

!!!

AND WHAT HAPPENED TO SISTER NAMI'S SISTER AND THAT MAN!?

BROTHER COOK'S NOT COMING UP!

THIS FOOL'S STILL NOT DEAD!?

...BREATHE WITH THEIR LUNGS ON LAND AND SWITCH TO GILLS IN THE WATER!! SO RIGHT NOW, HE'S JUST A TALKING FISH!!

ALL RIGHT THEN, WE'LL DO IT AGAIN !!!

THESE FISH-MEN...

FISH DIE WHEN AIR IS FORCED THROUGH THEIR GILLS!!

WE'RE NEAR THE SURFACE NOW. THINK YOU CAN SURVIVE A SECOND PLUNGE?

AND IT SHOULD BE THE SAME WITH HIM !!!

HALF!? HALF OF HIM. HE IS? DON'T WORRY... HE'S ALL RIGHT.

I'LL EXPLAIN LATER!!!

HUFF HUFF SHLUP!! PEG! SPLASH

HAAAAH!!! GASP!!! HAAGABAAAGAH!!!! SANJI!!

HAAAAAAH FWOOOO HAAAAH!!

HUH?

I'M GOING TO FINISH YOU!!!!

COME ON OUT HERE, YOU LOUSY FISH!!!

I'M MANY TIMES STRONGER THAN YOU ARE. IT DOESN'T MATTER IF WE'RE IN WATER OR OUT OF IT.

AND NOW YOU'VE MADE ME MAD.

KOFF!! YOU STILL DON'T UNDER-STAND. KOFF!!

SPLASHHH...!!

BUT MY GREATEST MOVE IS THE THOUSAND-BRICK FIST. THE LIKELIHOOD OF YOUR SURVIVAL IS...ZERO!!!

I SENT YOU FLYING BEFORE WITH THE HUNDRED-BRICK FIST.

WO OO

I'LL DESTROY YOU WITH THE ULTIMATE MOVE OF FISH-MAN KARATE.

COLLIER* COUP !!!

!

*COLLIER IS THE FRENCH TERM FOR "NECK MEAT."

*ÉPAULE = SHOULDER. (NOTE: THE ASTERISKS ON THIS PAGE INDICATE FRENCH WORDS.)

*SELLE = SADDLE (AS IN "SADDLE OF MUTTON")

*CÔTELETTE = BACK

*GIGOT = THIGH

*POITRINE = BREAST MEAT

*MOUTON = LAMB

Chapter 87:
IT'S ALL OVER!!

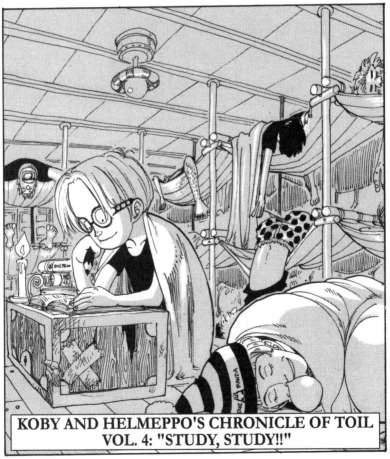

KOBY AND HELMEPPO'S CHRONICLE OF TOIL
VOL. 4: "STUDY, STUDY!!"

HACHI
...

KUROOBI
...

LOOKS LIKE WE'RE THE WINNERS OF THIS GAME.

DA-DOOM!!

LIKE I SAID, INSIGNIFICANT SMALL FRY.

KLAK

.....!!

HOW DARE YOU WIPE OUT MY MOST VALUABLE OFFICERS !?

WHO DO YOU THINK YOU ARE !!!?

I'LL HAVE TO GO BACK DOWN TO THE OCEAN FLOOR.

IT MEANS HE'S NOT DEAD... YET.

WHAT'S THAT MEAN?

YOU SAID LUFFY'S HALF-OKAY.

WHEEZE WHEEZE

KLAK

...THAT GUY ISN'T ABOUT TO LET ME.

BUT IT LOOKS LIKE...

THOSE GUYS ARE INCREDIBLE! THEY DEFEATED TWO OF ARLONG'S BEST MEN!!

......!!

HE'S COUGHING UP WATER. WE'RE SO CLOSE!

TAKE A BREAK, MR. GENZO!! I'LL GO DOWN NOW!!

HAAAH!! HAAAH!! THAT'S IT! I CAN'T HOLD MY BREATH ANY LONGER!!

huff

huff

GASP!

SPLASH!!

I STILL CAN HARDLY BELIEVE IT, BUT...

I WAS AFRAID TO BELIEVE IT UNTIL NOW.

NOBODY'S BEEN KILLED, YET!! IN FACT...

HOW'S IT GOING OVER THERE!?

huff

huff

... ABOUT THIS BATTLE !!!

I FEEL A RISING SENSE OF HOPE ...

DOOM!!

AND YOU WERE PRETTY FAST, FOR A HUMAN!!

BUT THEN YOU DIED FROM ONE SHOT OF MY LIP-O-BLASTER. HOW DISAPPOINTING.

DOOM!!

SMEK! ♡ YOU GAVE ME A HARD CHASE.

MY COMRADES SHOULD BE FINISHED BY NOW TOO.

TMP

TMP

GUESS I'LL HEAD BACK...

THAT GUY THINKS HE HIT ME WITH HIS *LIP-O-BLISTER* THING!! HEE HEE...JUST KEEP WALKING, LIPS!!

SUCCESS!! I'M SAVED!! GOOD THING I MADE THOSE KETCHUP STARS FOR JUST THIS KIND OF SITUATION!!

plip...

TMP

TMP

BA-BuMp

BLINK

BA-BuMp

BA-BuMp

I DO FEEL SORRY FOR NAMI...

...AND I WISH I COULD DO MORE TO HELP, BUT IF IT MEANS GETTING KILLED, I'LL PASS.

SHEESH, BUT WHAT A TERRIFYING SPECIES THEY ARE.

THEY CAN FLIP HOUSES UPSIDE DOWN! A WHOLE VILLAGE OF 'EM!!

tmp tmp

...THEN I MIGHT LOOK LIKE I FOUGHT A REAL BATTLE!

THAT'S IT! IF I SMEAR DIRT ALL OVER MYSELF...

...I WISH I HAD...A FEW MORE BATTLE SCARS!!

I'M COVERED WITH KETCHUP BLOOD, BUT...

WHAT SHOULD I SAY WHEN I GET BACK?

RUB

RUB

UMM, DON'T CRY, NAMI. IT WAS A HOPELESS BATTLE.

UMM, I ALMOST HAD HIM, BUT HE GOT AWAY.

WE'RE A TEAM, AREN'T WE?

UMM, SORRY. I LOST.

RUB

RUB

RUB

RUB

IT'S BUSINESS. I HAD NO CHOICE.

BUT HEY, COMPARED TO A BUNCH OF WOMAN-HATING CRAP PIRATES, HE'S NOT SO BAD!!

UMM, WELL, WE ALL PUT UP A GOOD FIGHT.

I PREFER DEATH TO DEFEAT.

UMM, WOW, THAT WAS ONE TOUGH FIGHT!

116

CAN YOU UNDERSTAND WHAT A PAINFUL CHOICE THAT WAS FOR HER?

WE'VE BEEN WAITING FOR YOU, BROTHERS!!!

UMM, MY WOUNDS AREN'T THAT BAD!!

.....!!

RUB...

RUB...

RUB...

RUB...

UMM, YOU SHOULDA SEEN ME FIGHT...

RUB...!!

LET'S FIGHT!!!

THIS IS SHAMEFUL!!!!

SWIP

SHAKE

SHAKE SHAKE

TOMP

LUFFY AND THOSE GUYS LIVE EVERY DAY LIKE THERE'S NO TOMORROW!!

YOU THINK I'D LET YOU HIT ME WITH YOUR WIMPY HALF-FISH SQUIRT GUN!!?

THE MOMENT I DECIDED TO LEAVE MY VILLAGE, I SAID GOODBYE TO PEACE AND SECURITY!!

SHAKE
SHAKE
SHAKE

BECAUSE I WANTED TO LAUGH WITH GUSTO, LIKE THEM !!!

ERK.... !

THAT'S THE REASON I SET OUT TO SEA IN THE FIRST PLACE!!

THAT'S WHY THEY CAN LAUGH SO HEARTILY!!

KR-EEEK!!!

HOW COULD I EVER LAUGH WITH THEM AGAIN !!?

DEATH BLOW !!

IF I DON'T FIGHT WITH EVERYTHING I'VE GOT...

...THEN I'M NOT WORTHY TO SAIL ON THE SAME SHIP WITH THOSE GUYS!!!

FW UMP...!!

YOUR BRAIN MUST BE AS WEAK AS YOUR BODY.

YOU SHOULD'VE JUST PLAYED DEAD.

SMEK. ♡

PLIP

PLIP.

THWAK THWAK

UNGH!!

AGH!

THWAK-THWAK THWAK!!

THAT'S RIGHT. IT'S ALL OVER FOR YOU!!!

IT'S ALL OVER.

twitch

twitch

...HAMMER!!!

USOPP'S...

WH TAK!!!

!!!

IT'S ALL OVER.

RUSTLE

SMEK?

KRAK...

OOF!!!

......

......!!

FLINCH!!

DOOM!!

SKREEK

USOPP'S RUBBER BAND OF DOOM!!!

...I'LL BLAST YOU WITH THE WATER FROM THIS PADDY!!!

SMEK. ♥

SHLURRG

BUT NO MATTER WHERE YOU'RE HIDING...

GRR!! THIS PUNY HUMAN IS FULL OF INSOLENT TRICKS!!

WHUP...!!

PLP...

SMEK. ♥

I'M A PIRATE NOW!!

IF I LOSE, I DIE!!

huff...

WHATEVER HAPPENS, I, USOPP, WILL NOT RUN FROM THIS FIGHT!!!

THAT FISH CAN SAY WHATEVER HE WANTS!

BOOM!!

LIP-O-CANNON!!!!

KA-BLOOSH!!!

KRAK
KRAK
KREK KREK···!!!

THWUMP!

WOW!!!

WHAT POWER!!!

DO————OM

SCARY

THERE HE IS.

WHY DO I HAVE TO FIGHT *THIS* FOOL?

Q: Sensei! I thought up a new technique for Luffy. He stretches his mouth and eats up his enemy and later flushes him down the toilet along with his *oop! What do you think? Good idea, huh?

A: It stinks-o.

Q: I've got a question for Oda Sensei. Whaddaya call Belle-Mère's hairdo?

A: It's called "women are brave." Go to the beauty parlor and shout it out.

Q: I'm glad that brother Sanji is a ladies' man and not a "gentlemen's man."

A: Indeed.

Q: When Sanji is thinking about a girl, his cigarette smoke forms the shape of a heart. How does he do that? I want to do that too!! Please (x100) teach me!

A: Hmm. First you have to be over 20 years old. Then light a cigarette and take a deep puff of smoke. Let the smoke soak up the feelings of love that you've prepared in your lungs and exhale it from your mouth. The smoke will surely come out in the shape of a heart.

Q: I can't quite decide whether Yosaku and Johnny are strong or not. I'm within a frog's hair of being able to tell. But really, between those two and Helmeppo, who will develop more?

A: I have high hopes that, one day, Kaya will become an excellent doctor.

Chapter 88:
DIE!!!

KOBY AND HELMEPPO'S CHRONICLE OF TOIL
VOL. 5: "CHORE BOYS ABOARD MORGAN'S PRISON SHIP!!"

HAMMER !!!!

SPLA———SH!!

SSSSS————SS!!

USOPP'S HAMMER !!

USOPP'S RUBBER BAND OF DOOM !!!

USOPP'S HAMMER !

USOPP'S HAMMER !

USOPP'S HAMMER !

!!!!?

WHY... YOU...

TWITCH!!

WHAM!

...

WHAK! BAM BAM!

!! .....

SWIP...!?

I'VE DONE MY CRYING!!

AND I'VE VOICED MY COMPLAINTS!!

KRK

UNH!!

MY MIND IS MADE UP!!

TMP TMP TMP TMPTMP...

...AND JOIN THE FIGHT!!!

I HAVE TO GO...

...BUT THEN THEY COUGHED UP BLOOD AND COLLAPSED!!

I DON'T KNOW. IT LOOKED LIKE HE JUST SPLASHED THEM WITH WATER...

WHOA... WHAT DID THAT NASTY SHARK DO?

WAS IT ALL A DREAM!?

GLUB GLUB

...!!

WHUMP

WHUMP

BREATHE!!

PLEASE...

SPLUP!!

WHAT'S HAPPENED TO BROTHER LUFFY!? HE COULDN'T HAVE DIED, COULD HE?

BROTHER COOK!! STAY DOWN!!

DID HE MOVE!?

JUST A LITTLE MORE!!!

TWITCH...

COME BACK TO LIFE!! PLEASE!!!

STAGGER...

.....

WHUMP!!!

WHUMP!!!

BUT HE'S LIKE A SHOTGUN BLAST!!! SO THIS IS THE POWER OF A SHARK...EVEN AMONG THE FISH-MEN, HE'S IN A CLASS BY HIMSELF!!

THIS GUY'S... NO JOKE!! HE MAKES IT LOOK EASY.

KOFF!

ACK!!!

YOUR LIVES ARE WORTH-LESS.

GO AHEAD AND DIE.

THIS IS LIKE NOTHING WE'VE FACED SO FAR!!

DO ZOOM

ARLONG !!!!

NAMI...

SISTER NAMI!!

WHAT BRINGS YOU HERE?

I WAS JUST ABOUT TO BLAST THIS NO-ACCOUNT PIRATE TO BITS.

MISS NAMI... ♡

NAMI...

...TO KILL YOU!!!

I'VE COME...

ASSASSINS... POISON... AMBUSHES...

...HOW MANY TIMES DID YOU TRY TO KILL ME?

......!!

BWAH HA HA HA HA!! BWAHHAHAHAHAHA

TO KILL ME!?

IN THE EIGHT YEARS YOU'VE BEEN WITH US...

YOU, OF ALL PEOPLE, SHOULD KNOW THAT NO MERE HUMAN CAN KILL ME!!!

AND THE RESULT!? I'M STILL HERE, AIN'T I!!?

!!!

SHIVER

YOU'RE GOING TO BE MY LITTLE CARTOGRAPHER FOREVER.

BUT I WON'T LET YOU GO!!!

NOW LISTEN. I'M NOT GOING TO KILL YOU...

I'D PREFER THAT YOU KEEP WORKING FOR ME OF YOUR OWN FREE WILL.

BUT I'M A REASONABLE FISH-MAN!

I DON'T WANT TO HOLD A YOUNG GIRL AGAINST HER WILL.

...IF YOU'RE WILLING TO REJOIN MY CREW...

...AND AGREE TO BE AN OFFICER AND DRAW OCEAN CHARTS...

...EXCEPT FOR YOU. HOWEVER...

NOW, I'M ABOUT TO KILL EVERY HUMAN HERE...

THEY'VE CAUSED ME TOO MUCH TROUBLE.

SO WHAT'S IT GONNA BE?

WHAK!

UNH...

BUT THESE TWO DIE, OF COURSE.

...I'M WILLING TO SPARE THE PEOPLE OF COCO VILLAGE.

...YOU CAN SEE WHAT A TRAGIC MISTAKE THAT WOULD BE!!

OR STICK WITH THESE WEAKLINGS AND TRY TO FIGHT ME TOGETHER!!

COME BACK TO ME NOW AND SAVE YOUR BELOVED VILLAGERS...

GULP....!!

BUT IF YOU LOOK AT THE SHAPE THESE TWO ARE IN...

ARE YOU MY SHIP-MATE...

WELL, NAMI!!?

...OR THEIRS?

BUT IF I SAY I'M ARLONG'S, ALL OF THE VILLAGERS WILL BE SPARED!! IS IT UP TO ME TO DECIDE WHO LIVES AND WHO DIES!!?

IF I SAY I'M LUFFY AND ZOLO'S SHIPMATE, EVERYONE MAY GET KILLED.

I HAVE TO BELIEVE IN THEM!!!

THAT'S DIRTY!! HE'S GONNA KEEP NAMI NO MATTER WHAT SHE DECIDES!!

....!!

BUT...I...

OKAY !!!!

...WITH ME!!!

FIGHT AND DIE...

I'M SORRY, EVERYONE !!!

142

DO OM!!

. . . . .

!

fwup!

ZOLO
...

!?

THAT'S PLENTY!!

SPLASH!!

!

THIRTY SECONDS!! I WON'T LAST MORE THAN THAT.

CHOMP

COULD IT BE THAT RUBBER BRAT!!?

ARLONG PARK HAS NO FOUNTAINS!

146

THERE YOU ARE!!!

FIGHT ALL YOU LIKE!!!

THWUMP!

I'VE GOT YOUR BACK, ZOLO!!!

HE'S ALIVE!? BUT WHERE IS HE!? WHAT A DRAMATIC ENTRANCE!!

BROTHER USOPP!? HOW BRAVE!!

CAN'T YOU USE YOUR STRENGTH TO FREE YOURSELF SOMEHOW!?

D-O-OM!

NOPE. NO CAN DO. I'M JUST TOO WEAK.

DOOM!!

huff huff huff !!

NAMI!!!! I BEAT... I BEAT... I BEAT ONE OF ARLONG'S OFFICERS! ME!!!

USOPP!!

YOU THINK I'D LET YOU HUMANS WIN!?

FWUP...

THWOOM!!

GLUB

I'M COUNTING ON YOU.

YOU'RE OUR LAST HOPE.

GLUB

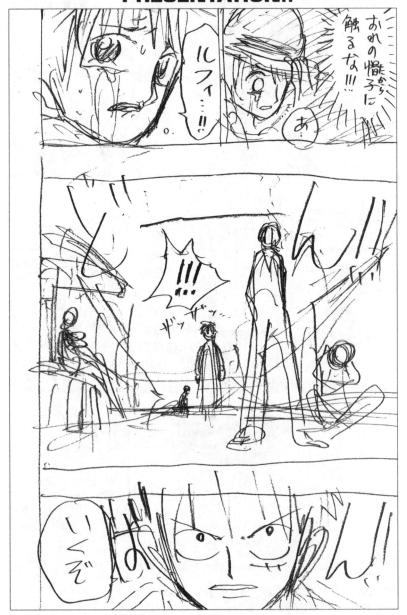

Chapter 89:
TRADE-OFF

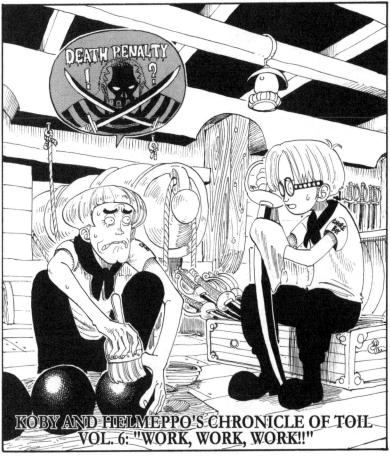

KOBY AND HELMEPPO'S CHRONICLE OF TOIL
VOL. 6: "WORK, WORK, WORK!!"

HE'S THE ONLY ONE LEFT WITH ANY HOPE OF BEATING ARLONG!!!

IF I CAN JUST KICK THE ROCK AROUND LUFFY'S LEGS TO PIECES, HE CAN SWING INTO ACTION!!!

GLUB GLUB GLUB

BROTHER ZOLO!! HOLD FAST!!

IT'S BROTHER COOK!!! I DON'T KNOW WHAT HE'S DOING DOWN THERE, BUT WE'RE ALL COUNTING ON HIM NOW!!!

SO IF THAT BRAT IS STILL ALIVE, THEN SOMEONE...

...MUST BE HELPING HIM!!!

...BUT THE OCEAN ALSO TAKES AWAY THEIR WILL TO LIVE.

NOT ONLY DO PEOPLE WITH DEVIL-FRUIT POWERS LOSE THEM UNDER-WATER...

SPLA·SH·!!

I'LL KILL THAT SHIPMATE OF YOURS WHO'S IN THE OCEAN !!!

I WON'T LET YOU FOOLS WIN...

...RORONOA ZOLO!!!

DIE !!!!

DON'T WORRY ABOUT IT. IN THE END, YOU'RE ALL GOING TO...

...!!!

BROTHER ZOLO !!!!

SHUNK !!!

AAARGH !!!

LEAVE THE REST TO ME!!!

FWUP

GLUB

GLUB

!

GET BACK!!! I CAN SHATTER THAT ROCK.

GLUB...!!

A FISH-MAN!

!!

JUST ONE GOOD KICK!!!

WHOOM!!

DIE!! DIE!!!

RRMMMBB

HEH HEH...

WHEEZE

EH?

...FINISH HIM OFF RIGHT NOW!!!

I'D BETTER...

...WOULD'VE KEPT SOME OF THE WOUNDS FROM OPENING UP!!!

·····

LYING STILL...

HUFF HUFF

!

I MEANT OCTOPUS BOY.

I WASN'T TALKING ABOUT ME!!

IS THAT YOUR IDEA OF A JOKE?

YOU'RE PROBABLY RIGHT.

HUH!!!?

I TOLD YOU. THIS IS OUR GAME... AND WE'RE WINNING.

WHAT!?

PLOO

!!?

S

GRAAAAR!!!!

THAT WAS CLOSE!!!

KA-BAM!!!!

WHOA. ...!!

blup blup...

IT'S THE RUBBER BOY!!!

PHEW...

.....!!!

LUFFY!!

BROTHER LUFFY!!!

IDIOT!!!

IT'S ABOUT TIME...

THE RUBBER BOY.

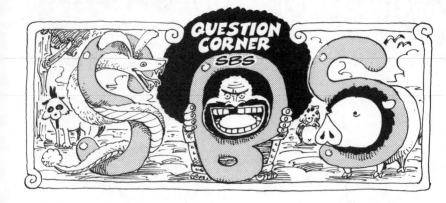

Q: After reading your manga, Sensei, I'm inspired to follow my dream. My dream is to build a big bridge in America.

A: That's nice. A young man with dreams. I like that. All right then, do it. And if anyone gets in your way I'll go and--wearing hard leather boots--stomp on the pinky toe of his foot, so don't worry. Go for it.

Q: Knock, knock, Oda Sensei. Oda-body home!!?

A: Give me a break.

Q: When Patty the Cook says "I'm turniply saucy," what does it mean?

A: "I'm terribly sorry." He tends to make things sound like food. For example, he might say: "He's quite a man. He did lettuce of ham-glazing a-cheese-mints. Peas apple-aud him." But if *you* say things like that, people will probably look at you funny.

Q: A question for you. Is there a bone in Usopp's nose? I've seen it bend so many times. Like *squish*.

A: I've never seen that. Bend...like *squish*? How absurd...

Whoa!! It does bend!!!
Here ends SBS!!

Chapter 90:
WHAT CAN YOU DO?

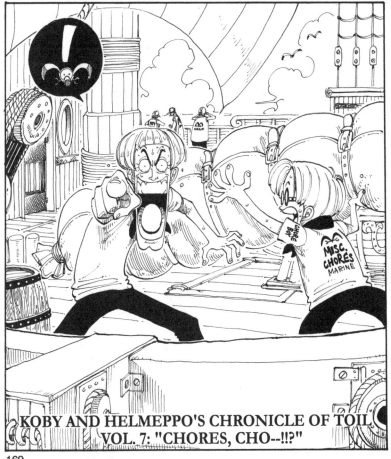

KOBY AND HELMEPPO'S CHRONICLE OF TOIL, VOL. 7: "CHORES, CHO--!!?"

BUT YOU'D HAVE BEEN BETTER OFF DYING PEACEFULLY AT THE BOTTOM OF THE OCEAN.

HA HA HA HA HA... HOW TENACIOUSLY YOU SCUM HOLD ON BY YOUR STUBBY LITTLE TEETH.

UNH!!

UNH!!

WOING WOING

CAN'T YOU UNDERSTAND WHY I'M UPSET?

I'M GLAD THEY RESCUED ME.

UNH!!

I'LL SOON MAKE YOU WISH FOR A QUIET DEATH.

I'VE WATCHED MY BELOVED COMRADES BE DEFEATED BY WORMS!!!

HEY, WHERE DID BROTHER ZOLO FLY OFF TO!?

ALL OF HIS FEROCIOUS ATTACKS DIDN'T EVEN SEEM TO FAZE ARLONG!!

IS BROTHER LUFFY ALL RIGHT?

.....

FWIK

FWIK

FWIK

BIG DEAL.

THWUMP!

GO, LUFFY!! I'VE GOT YOUR BACK!!

KROOSH SPLASH

YOU'RE RIGHT.

THAT WOULD BE THE END OF THE EAST BLUE.

IF LUFFY LOSES, WE'RE ALL DEAD.

WHUP

OUR NOSES.

krak krak

DO YOU KNOW THE DIFFERENCE BETWEEN YOU AND ME?

OUR CHINS?

DOOM

WEBBED TOES !!?

I... I THINK HE'S SERIOUS.

IS BROTHER LUFFY JOKING !?

CHOMP !!!

HUP.

NO... SPECIES !!!!

CHOK !! CHOK !! CHOK !! CHONK !!

OOF! UNH! OH! WAH!

GRAAR !!

KRAS

WAAAAAAH!!! HE CHEWED UP THAT STONE PILLAR!!!

WOW!! SCARY!

THOOM!!

HE'LL BE EATEN UP, BONES AND ALL!!

AAAAAAH

...!?

IF THOSE JAWS CLAMP ONTO LUFFY, THEY WON'T JUST LEAVE MARKS.

FROM THE MOMENT OF BIRTH, AN UNBRIDGEABLE GULF SEPARATES OUR SPECIES !!!

SUPER-HUMAN STRENGTH IS THE BIRTHRIGHT OF ALL FISH-MEN.

YOU'RE INHERENTLY INFERIOR!!!

THE HEAVENS DIDN'T SMILE ON YOUR PUNY KIND IN THAT REGARD.

...

YOU SINK LIKE ROCKS IN THE OCEAN!!! WHAT CAN YOU DO !!?

HUMANS ARE A STUPID, WEAK, FOOLISH SPECIES !!!

...BUT I HAVE FRIENDS WHO WILL RESCUE ME!!!

MAYBE I CAN'T DO ANY-THING...

DOES HE EVEN KNOW HOW TO USE A SWORD?

SHOO!!

.....

FWOOS

UNH!!!

KLAK KLAK

KLAK...!!!

ENOUGH FOOLISH-NESS.

CLENCH YOUR TEETH!!!

FWRRR...

WHOOSH

KA-

PO

!!!?

W

KREESI

GRAAH!!!!

KR EK

WHAT !!?

HE SHATTERED ARLONG'S TEETH !!!!

GWAAAAH !!!

HUH? WHAT'S HE ON ABOUT?

THOOM

SPLASH!

I DON'T KNOW HOW TO USE A SWORD, SHARK FACE !!!

DOOM!

AN ENDLESS NUMBER OF TIMES!!!

AN ENDLESS NUMBER OF TIMES!!!

SHEENK

WOW.

THIS IS A SPECIAL POWER BESTOWED BY THE GODS.

•••••

CHOMP!!!

...HOW SUPERIOR WE FISH-MEN ARE?

NOW DO YOU SEE...

TO BE CONTINUED IN **ONE PIECE**, VOL. 11!

COMING NEXT VOLUME:

Luffy's fun idea makes him more than an ideal match for the toothsome Captain Arlong. During a brief lull in their pitched battle, Luffy learns the unhappy tale behind Arlong Park's map room and takes it upon himself to demolish it completely, along with Arlong Park itself!

ON SALE NOW!

NARUTO

Story and Art by
Masashi Kishimoto

Naruto is determined to become the greatest ninja ever!

Twelve years ago the Village Hidden in the Leaves was attacked by a fearsome threat. A nine-tailed fox spirit claimed the life of the village leader, the Hokage, and many others. Today, the village is at peace and a troublemaking kid named Naruto is struggling to graduate from Ninja Academy. His goal may be to become the next Hokage, but his true destiny will be much more complicated. The adventure begins now!

WORLD'S BEST SELLING MANGA!

www.shonenjump.com

www.viz.com

You're Reading in the Wrong Direction!!

Whoops! Guess what? You're starting at the wrong end of the comic!

...It's true! In keeping with the original Japanese format, **One Piece** is meant to be read from right to left, starting in the upper-right corner.

Unlike English, which is read from left to right, Japanese is read from right to left, meaning that action, sound effects and word-balloon order are completely reversed... something which can make readers unfamiliar with Japanese feel pretty backwards themselves. For this reason, manga or Japanese comics published in the U.S. in English have sometimes been published "flopped" – that is, printed in exact reverse order, as though seen from the other side of a mirror.

By flopping pages, U.S. publishers can avoid confusing readers, but the compromise is not without its downside. For one thing, a character in a flopped manga series who once wore in the original Japanese version a T-shirt emblazoned with "M A Y" (as in "the merry month of") now wears one which reads "Y A M"! Additionally, many manga creators in Japan are themselves unhappy with the process, as some feel the mirror-imaging of their art skews their original intentions.

We are proud to bring you Eiichiro Oda's **One Piece** in the original unflopped format. For now, though, turn to the other side of the book and let the journey begin...!

—Editor